DETECTING DISASTERS

DETECTING FLOODS

by Marne Ventura

FOCUS
READERS

WWW.NORTHSTAREDITIONS.COM

Produced for North Star Editions by Red Line Editorial.

Photographs ©: Phil MacD Photography/Shutterstock Images, cover, 1; Jonathan Bachman/ AP Images, 4–5; Pattie Calfy/iStockphoto, 7; Max Becherer/AP Images, 8; aerogondo2/ Shutterstock Images, 10–11; LaiQuocAnh/Shutterstock Images, 13; NASA, 15; Dewitt/ Shutterstock Images, 16–17; Marcin Szymczak/Shutterstock Images, 19; Zern Liew/ Shutterstock Images, 20–21; Jim Reed/Science Source, 22–23; Erik Simonsen/Getty Images, 25; US Army, 27

Content Consultant: William Gallus, Professor, Department of Geological and Atmospheric Sciences, Iowa State University

ISBN
978-1-63517-002-3 (hardcover)
978-1-63517-058-0 (paperback)
978-1-63517-164-8 (ebook pdf)
978-1-63517-114-3 (hosted ebook)

Library of Congress Control Number: 2016949780

Printed in the United States of America
Mankato, MN
November, 2016

ABOUT THE AUTHOR

Marne Ventura is the author of 41 books for kids. She loves writing about nature, science, technology, food, health, and crafts. She is a former elementary school teacher and holds a master's degree in education from the University of California.

TABLE OF CONTENTS

CHAPTER 1

THE WATER'S RISING!

Dennis Easter drove toward home. It was a rainy morning in May 2015. By this time, the heavy rains had been falling for a week. Easter had gone to get sandbags. He planned to use them to build a wall around his house. He hoped to stop water from washing away his property.

If sandbags are put in place soon enough, they can protect homes from flood damage.

Easter's family had lived next to the Cache Creek in Oklahoma for more than 40 years. They had been through a flood in 2007. Easter knew that in a storm, the creek could rise quickly and cause a lot of damage.

Easter's phone rang. It was his grown daughter, Cindy. She sounded scared. She urged him to get home fast. Easter told her to hang on and try not to panic. He would be there as soon as he could.

When he got home, he saw that it was too late for sandbags. The water was rising fast. Easter saw Cindy on the patio. He jumped from the car and ran to her. The water was rushing across the porch.

Flooding can make roads and sidewalks extremely dangerous.

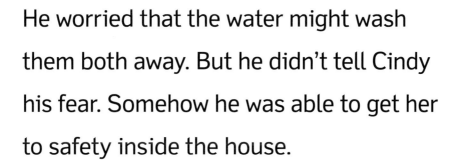

He worried that the water might wash them both away. But he didn't tell Cindy his fear. Somehow he was able to get her to safety inside the house.

Now Easter had to find his wife, Katey. The water was 4 feet (1.2 m) deep.

Boats are often used to rescue people trapped by rising floodwaters.

He found Katey inside the house, sitting on top of the washing machine.

The moving water had left a huge log leaning against the porch. Easter broke open the kitchen window so they could get out of the house. They climbed onto the roof, using the log as a ladder.

Happy to be alive, the dripping-wet family sat atop the house and waited for rescue.

At 2:30 a.m., a young man in a small fishing boat picked up the Easters. The family hugged each other in relief. Although their house was ruined, they were safe and together. They had survived a devastating flood.

SOUTHERN PLAINS FLOODS

Rainfall in Texas and Oklahoma set a new record high in May 2015. One storm after another hit these areas. Rivers and lakes overflowed, and people had to leave their homes. Roads had to be closed because they were underwater. Arkansas, Kansas, and Louisiana also experienced flooding.

CHAPTER 2

THE SCIENCE OF FLOODS

People, plants, and animals on Earth need water to live. Most of the planet is covered with water. When the sun heats the water, some of the water **evaporates**. The water rises, cools, and forms clouds. When the water droplets in clouds grow big enough, they become raindrops and fall back down to the planet's surface.

Heavy rain falling into rivers is one of the main causes of floods.

The movement of water back and forth between the surface and the **atmosphere** is called the water cycle.

Falling rain enters oceans, lakes, and rivers. It may also flow on the surface and soak into the ground. Flooding occurs when an area gets more water than it can handle. Storms can bring too much rain. Melting snow in the spring can dump extra water into a river. When this happens, rivers overflow. The soil can't soak up any more water. Water collects and flows on the surface.

The flat lands along the sides of rivers are called floodplains. When rivers overflow, these strips of land hold the

Melting snow can fill up rivers and cause flooding downstream.

water. Because floodplains are usually dry, people often build cities there. Being near the river is useful most of the time. Rivers make travel and trade easy.

But these cities are at risk when floods happen.

Deltas are land areas where a river empties its water into the ocean. **Sediment** builds up in deltas. This makes the soil very **fertile**. People who live in deltas are at risk for floods.

CITIES IN FLOODPLAINS AND DELTAS

Throughout history, towns and cities have sprung up near water for many reasons. People need clean water to live. The fertile soil in deltas and floodplains is good for farming. Traders use boats to send goods to other places. And the land is easier to build on because it is flat.

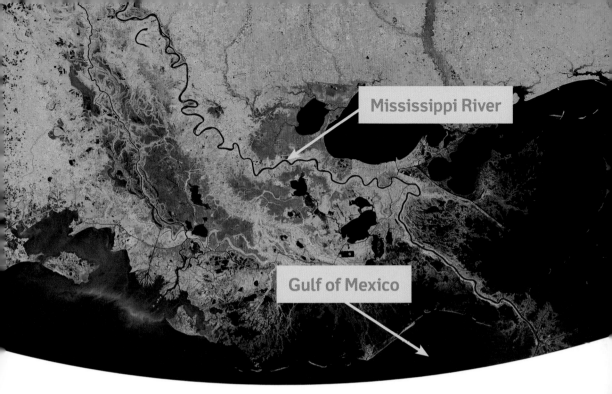

Mississippi River

Gulf of Mexico

This satellite image shows where the Mississippi River empties into the Gulf of Mexico.

Some floods happen slowly, after many days of rain. Flash floods occur quickly, in a few hours or less. Heavy rains brought by severe storms or hurricanes can cause flash floods. Other times flash floods happen because a **dam** or **levee** breaks.

CHAPTER 3

TAKING ACTION AGAINST FLOODS

People build levees to prevent floods. Levees are barriers built along the sides of a river. They are usually made of soil. They raise the banks of the river so it will hold more water. This stops the water from flowing over into nearby towns. The Mississippi River has levee systems built along its banks in some areas.

When levees work properly, they can protect wide areas from flooding.

Dams are another way that people control the flow of water. Dams are walls built in rivers. They are often made of concrete or soil. They slow the water's flow. This forms a lake, or reservoir, behind the wall. Dams can prevent flooding. Sometimes they also use the force of flowing water to create electricity.

Government officials send out flood warnings when they know a storm might cause flooding. People in high-risk areas can check the Internet, television, and radio for information. This gives them time to prepare. They might want to put

Dams allow people to collect, store, and control huge amounts of water.

sandbags around their homes or move to a higher place.

If the flood risk is high, officials might tell people to **evacuate**. Officials can warn people that certain areas, such as deserts, are more likely to have flash floods in a sudden rainstorm.

TYPES OF DAMS

Arch dam: An arch dam is built inside a canyon. Water pushing against the curved wall holds the dam in place.

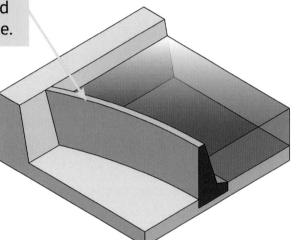

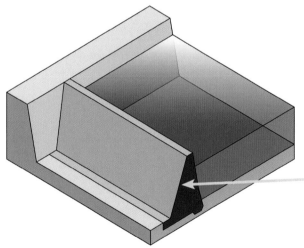

Gravity dam: A gravity dam is a concrete dam that is thicker and heavier on the bottom. This keeps the weight of the water from making the dam tip over.

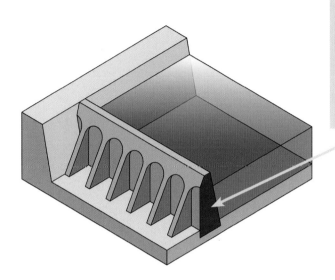

Buttress dam: A buttress dam has supports on the outside that push back against the weight of the water.

Embankment dam: An embankment dam is made of a thick earthen wall. Engineers use soil that does not absorb water.

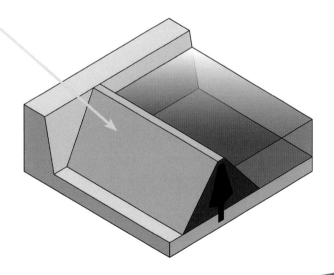

CHAPTER 4

DETECTION AND PREDICTION

Meteorologists are scientists who study weather. They use computers, **radar**, and other technology. They look for weather patterns. They make predictions about storms, hurricanes, and floods.

One way that meteorologists predict floods is by using radar. Radar tells scientists where rain is falling.

Radar data helps meteorologists figure out where floods might happen.

Radar also shows which way the wind is blowing and how fast a storm is moving. Meteorologists track the path of the storm. This lets them predict where the storm will go next so they can warn people who may be in its path.

Scientists also use weather satellites to detect floods. Satellites orbit Earth. They take photos of the atmosphere.

DOPPLER RADAR

To track storms, Doppler radar stations send out radio waves that bounce off rain, hail, or snow. Scientists can measure how long it takes the waves to return. The technology is named for Austrian scientist Christian Doppler.

Satellites track floods and other dangerous weather events.

Meteorologists use this information to predict floods.

Computer models are another way to predict flooding. Scientists feed data from radar and satellites into computers. The scientists add data about how much water a floodplain can absorb. They also factor in how heavy a rainfall or snowmelt is. A computer program combines all this data into a model of the situation. Scientists can use this model to find the **probability** of a flood in a certain area.

Computers also help engineers design stronger dams and levees. Engineers use math to figure out the best shape, weight, and height for these structures.

Designing and building new dams is one way to reduce flood risks.

They use data to find the safest places to put them. They also use computers to monitor the structures after they are built.

Scientists can often predict and detect floods. With enough warning, people can protect their homes or evacuate to dry areas. Floods may damage property, but detecting them early can help keep people safe.

FLOOD SAFETY CHECKLIST

- Do not walk through floodwaters. Just 6 inches (15 cm) of water can knock you off your feet.

- Prepare a flood emergency kit, including a flashlight, batteries, food, clean drinking water, and first aid supplies.

- If your house is at risk of flooding, move important items to the highest floor to protect them.

- If a flood watch is announced, there is a chance that flooding could occur. Check the Internet, television, or radio for updates.

- If a flood warning is announced, flooding has already started or will start soon. Move to higher ground right away.

- If local officials order an evacuation, follow their instructions to reach safety as soon as possible.

- Return to your home only after officials say the area is safe.

- After a flood, be extremely cautious and watch out for debris, downed power lines, and other dangers.

FOCUS ON
DETECTING FLOODS

Write your answers on a separate piece of paper.

1. Write a letter to a friend describing what you learned about ways to prevent floods from happening.

2. Do you think people should build cities on flood plains? Why or why not?

3. What is the water behind a dam called?

    A. a reservoir
    B. a delta
    C. a flood plain

4. What do sandbags and dams have in common?

    A. They can both be used to generate electricity.
    B. They can both be used to block flood waters.
    C. They can both be built quickly to protect a house.

Answer key on page 32.

GLOSSARY

atmosphere
The layer of air that surrounds Earth.

dam
A wall that stops water from flowing.

evacuate
To remove people from a place of danger.

evaporates
Changes from liquid to gas.

fertile
Good for growing plants.

levee
A structure built next to a river to stop floods.

probability
The chance something will happen.

radar
An instrument that locates things by bouncing radio waves off them.

sediment
Stones, sand, or other material that is carried by a river's rushing waters.

TO LEARN MORE

BOOKS

Davis, Graeme. *Floods.* Ann Arbor, MI: Cherry Lake, 2012.

Marquardt, Meg. *The Science of a Flood.* Ann Arbor, MI: Cherry Lake, 2016.

Mattern, Joanne. *Floods, Dams, and Levees.* Vero Beach, FL: Rourke, 2012.

NOTE TO EDUCATORS

Visit **www.focusreaders.com** to find lesson plans, activities, links, and other resources related to this title.

INDEX

Answer Key: 1. Answers will vary; **2.** Answers will vary; **3.** A; **4.** B